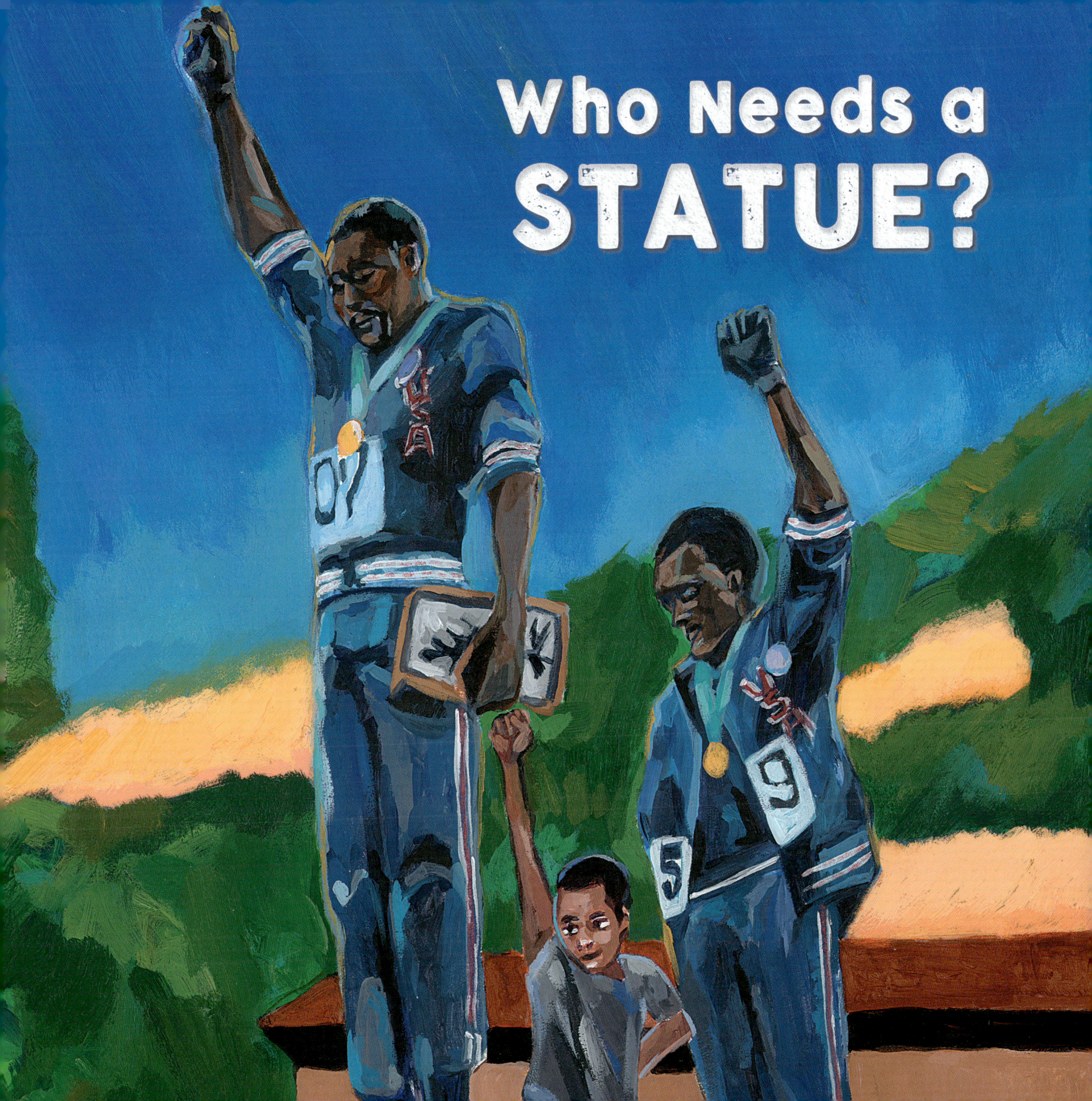

Who Needs a STATUE?

To Rose, Clara, Charlotte, and Philip
—EL

Many thanks to Susan Bulba Carvutto for introducing
me to Eve at the Bailey Library in Winthrop, Maine.
—MBK

To my parents, Joseph and Elina Delinois,
I love you both. Thank you for all the love
and sacrifices you made for our family.
See you soon!!!
—AD

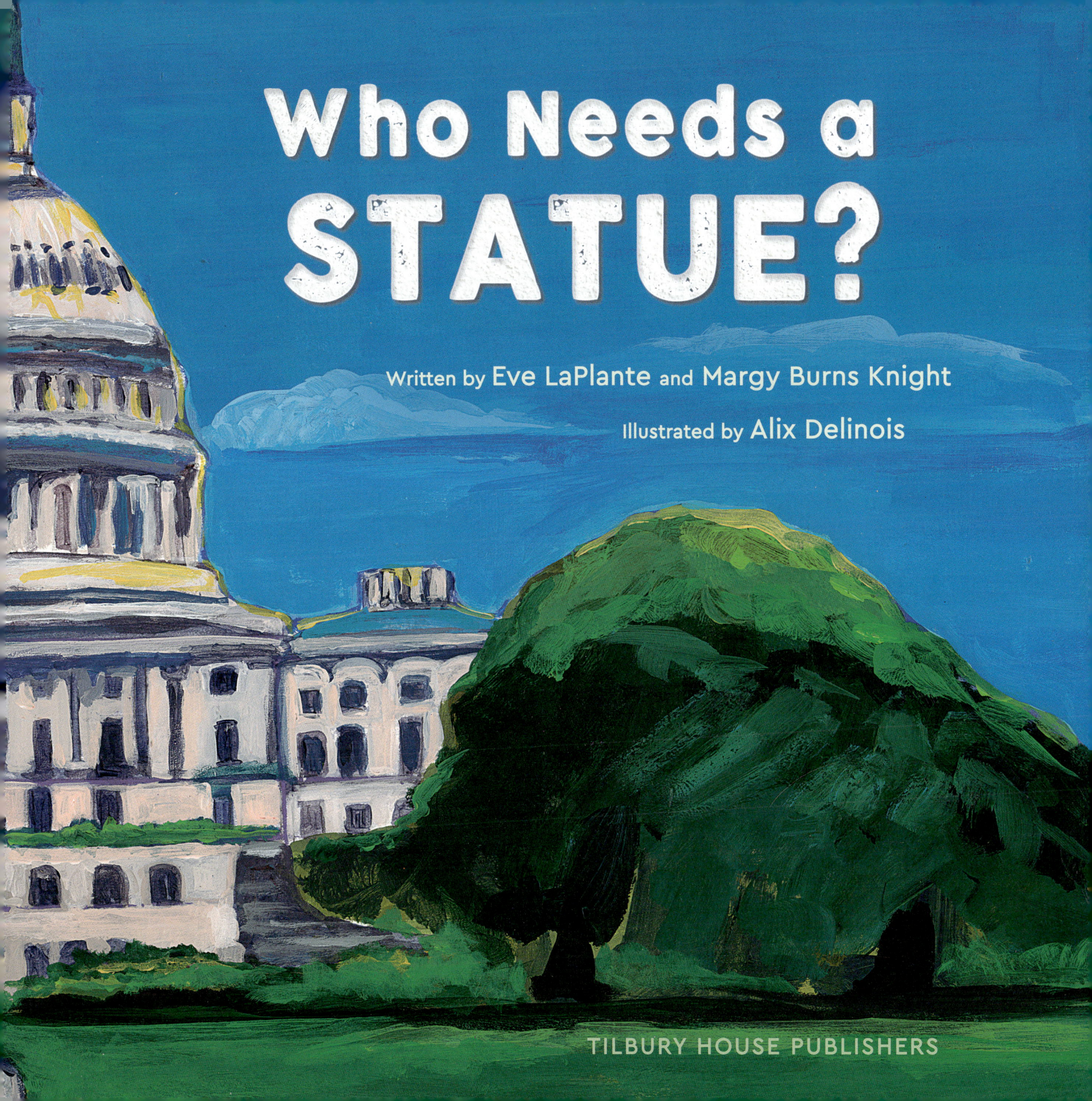

Who Needs a
STATUE?

Written by Eve LaPlante and Margy Burns Knight

Illustrated by Alix Delinois

TILBURY HOUSE PUBLISHERS

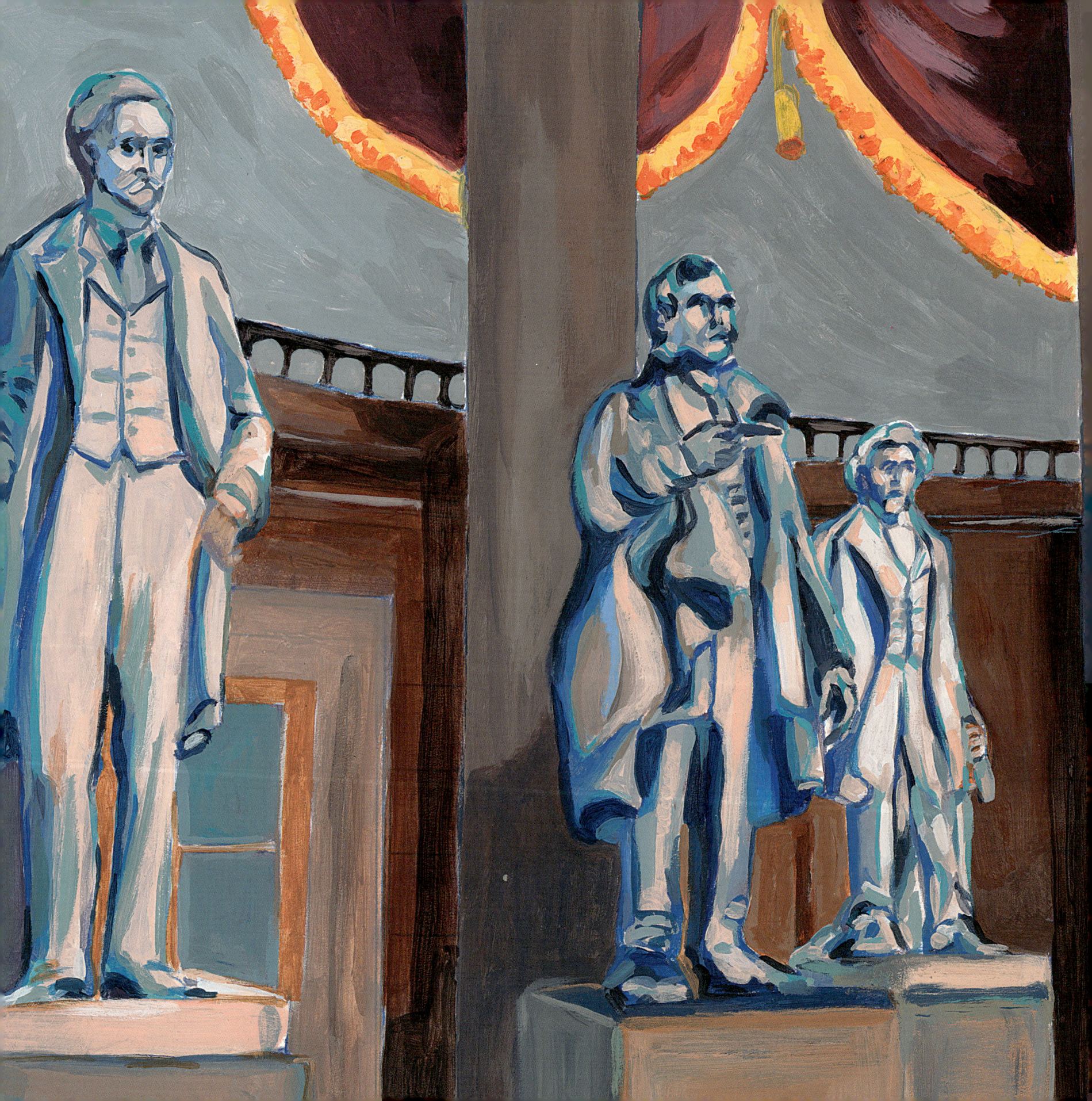

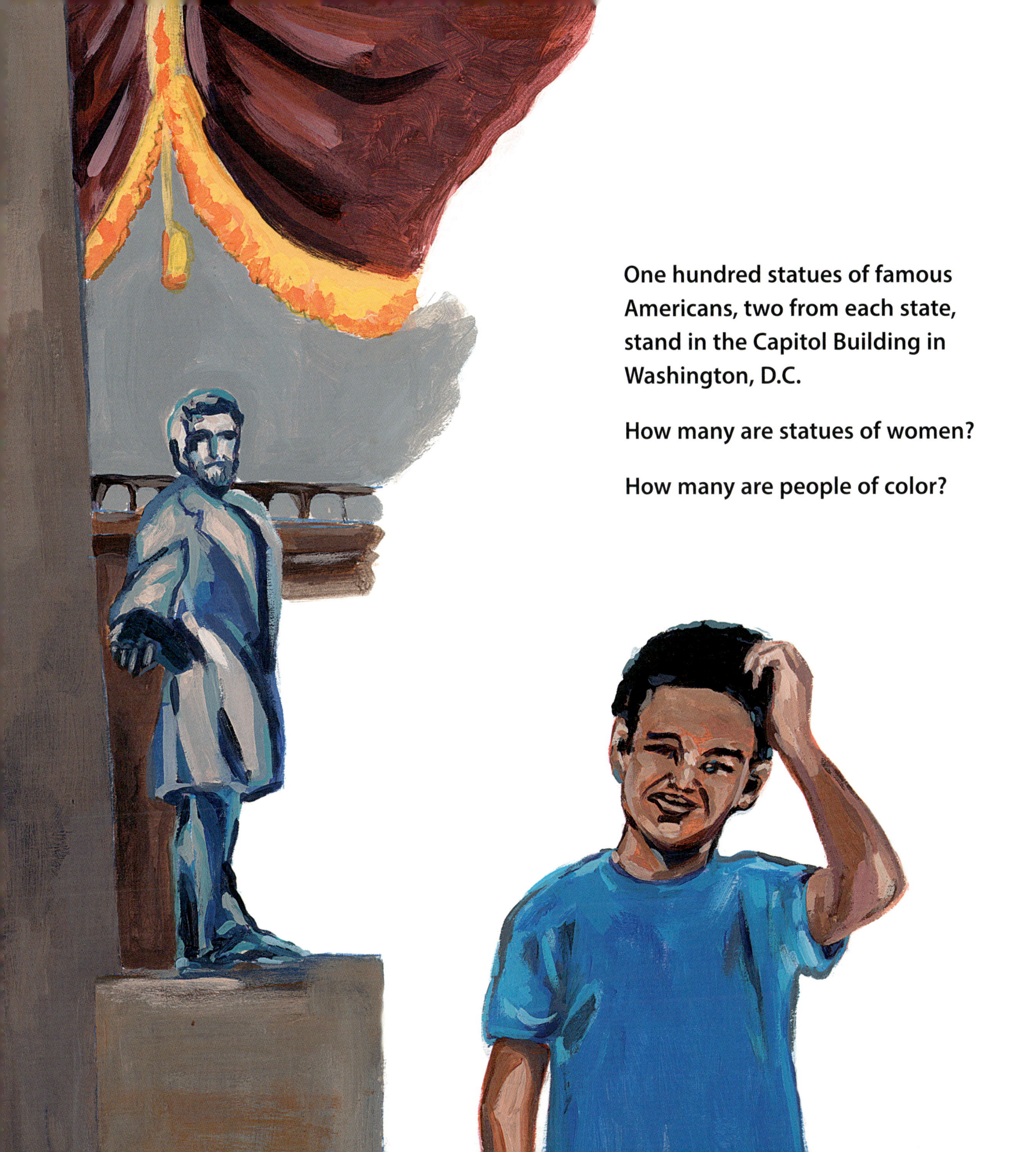

One hundred statues of famous Americans, two from each state, stand in the Capitol Building in Washington, D.C.

How many are statues of women?

How many are people of color?

Thocmetony Sarah Winnemucca holds her book *Life Among the Paiutes*.

She grew up in Nevada and spoke five languages by the time she was fourteen. Her 1883 autobiography was the first book published by a Native American woman.

King Kamehameha I holds his spear and welcomes his people.

Kamehameha was a brave warrior from Hawaii. He unified the islands and brought peace to indigenous Hawaiians. In 1810 he became Hawaii's first king.

Twelve of the 100 statues are women.

Jeannette Rankin carries a prayer asking for wisdom and courage.

From the state of Montana, Jeannette was the first woman elected to the United States Congress. That was in 1916, before most women could even vote.

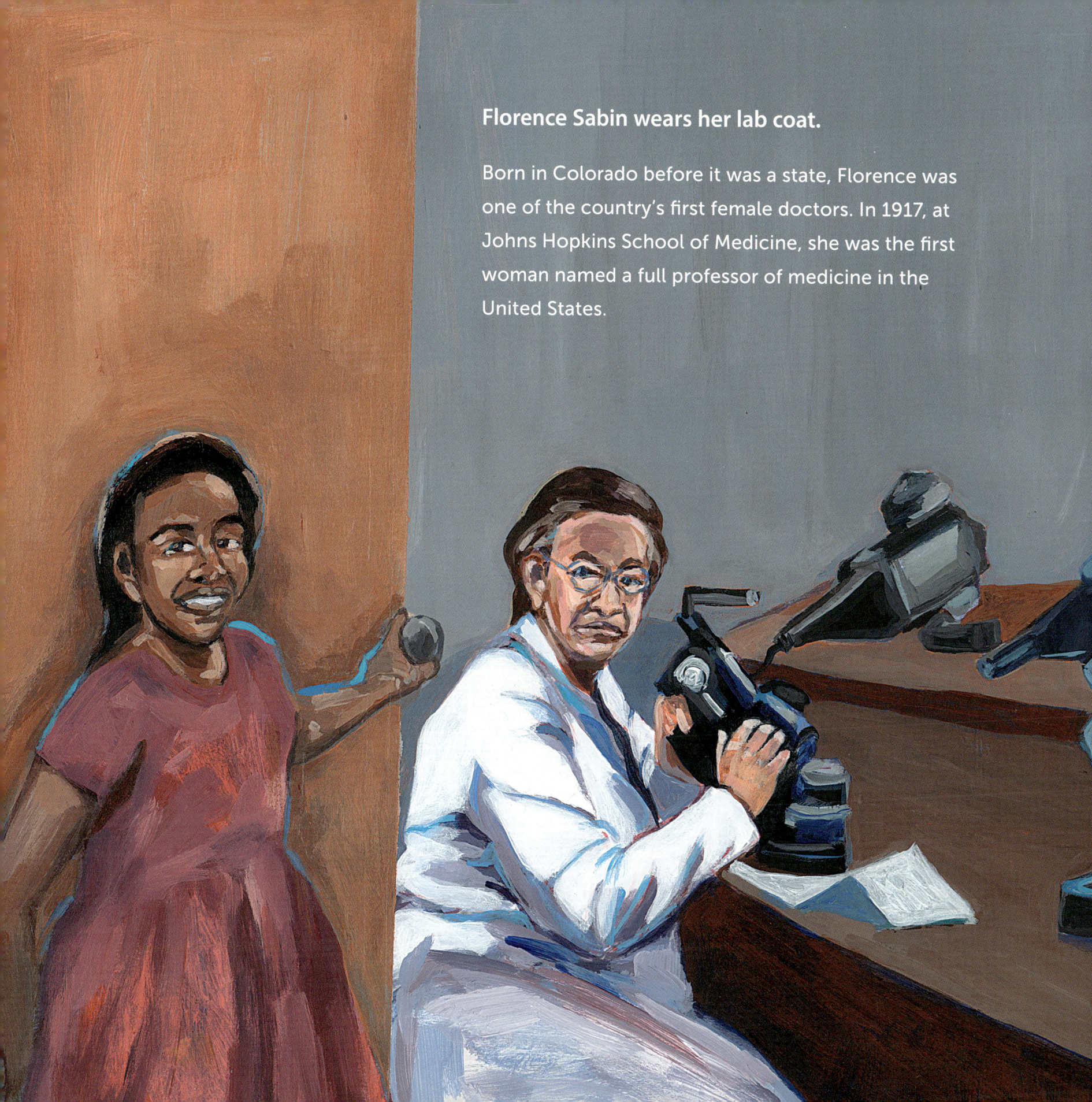

Florence Sabin wears her lab coat.

Born in Colorado before it was a state, Florence was one of the country's first female doctors. In 1917, at Johns Hopkins School of Medicine, she was the first woman named a full professor of medicine in the United States.

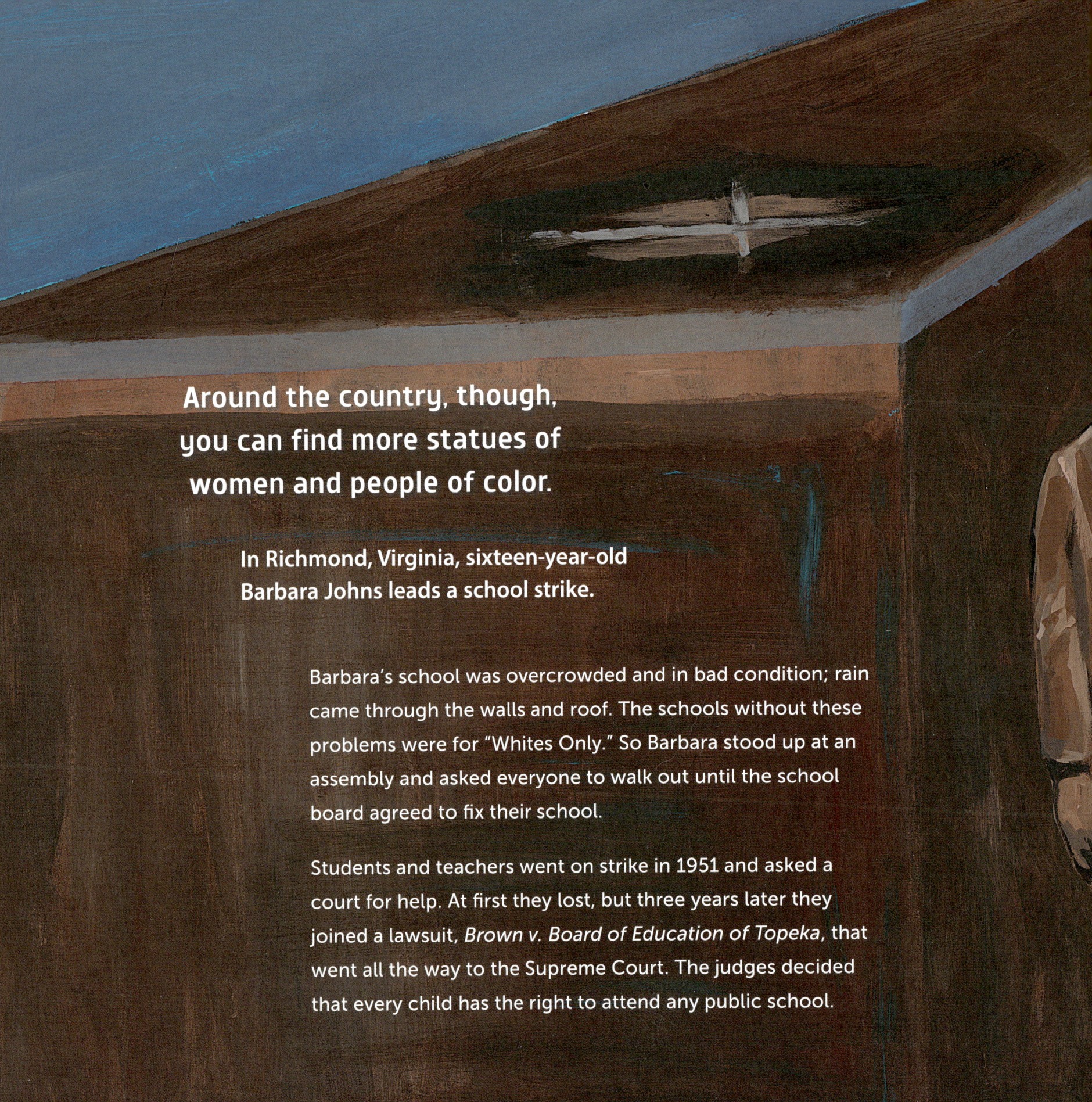

Around the country, though,
you can find more statues of
women and people of color.

In Richmond, Virginia, sixteen-year-old
Barbara Johns leads a school strike.

Barbara's school was overcrowded and in bad condition; rain
came through the walls and roof. The schools without these
problems were for "Whites Only." So Barbara stood up at an
assembly and asked everyone to walk out until the school
board agreed to fix their school.

Students and teachers went on strike in 1951 and asked a
court for help. At first they lost, but three years later they
joined a lawsuit, *Brown v. Board of Education of Topeka*, that
went all the way to the Supreme Court. The judges decided
that every child has the right to attend any public school.

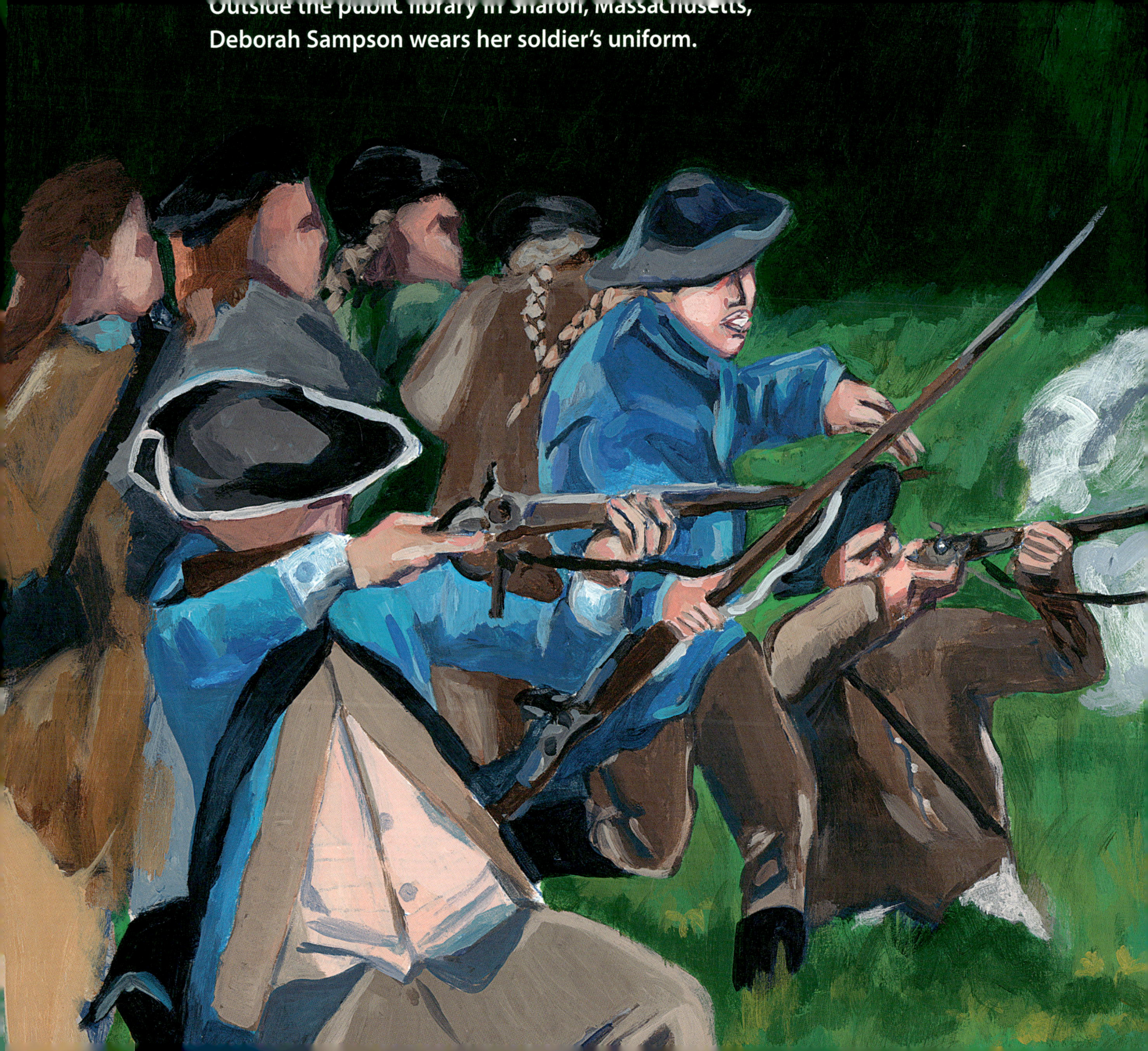

Outside the public library in Sharon, Massachusetts,
Deborah Sampson wears her soldier's uniform.

Fifteen-year-old Deborah wanted to fight in the Revolutionary War. Girls were not allowed to be soldiers, so she pretended to be a boy, put on an Army uniform, and reported for duty as a recruit named Robert.

She helped lead a raid and was wounded in battle in 1782. Deborah used a penknife to remove the musket ball from her thigh, and closed the wound with needle and thread. She recovered and was promoted. After the war she was honorably discharged from the Army. No one had discovered her secret.

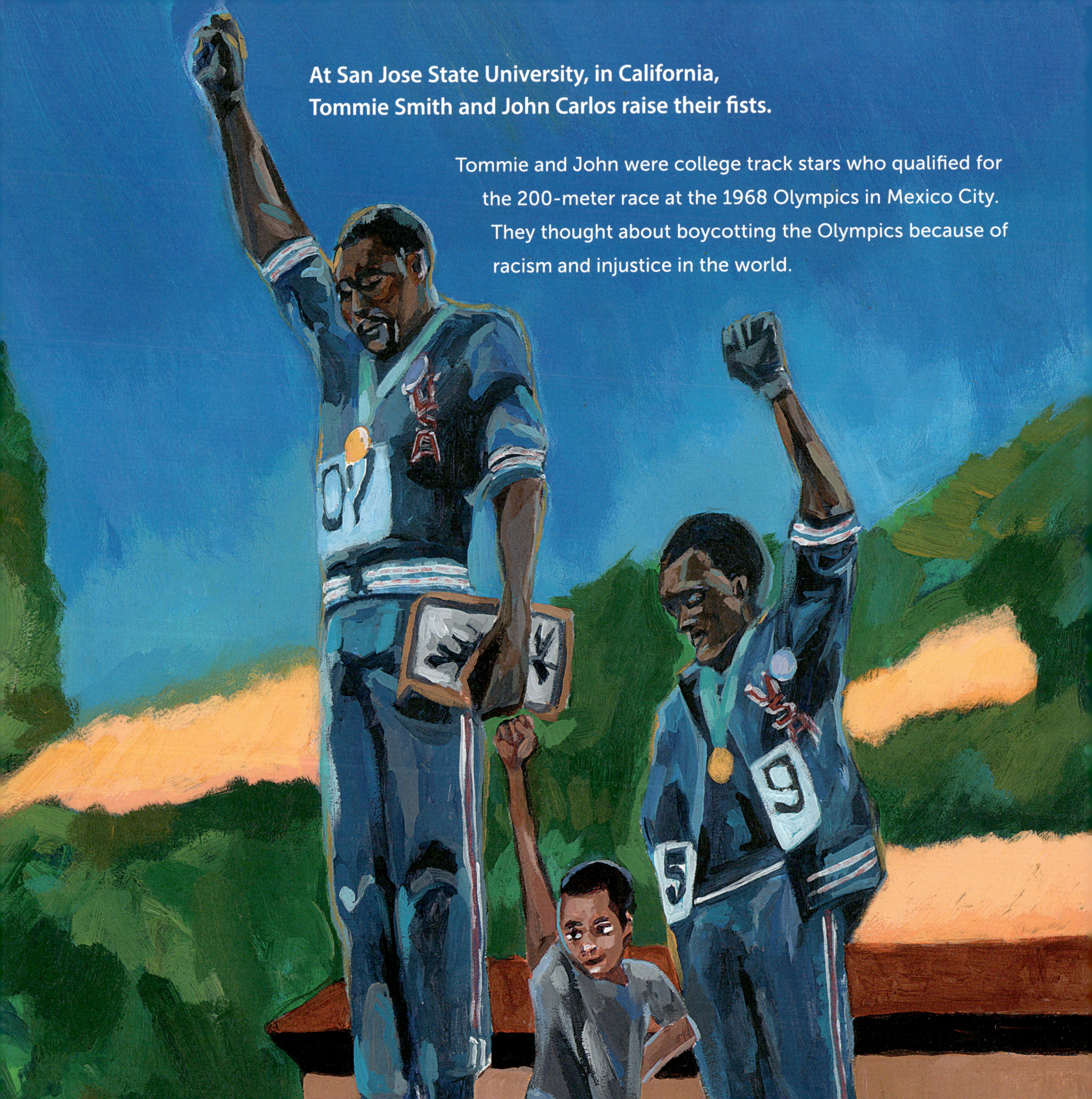

At San Jose State University, in California,
Tommie Smith and John Carlos raise their fists.

Tommie and John were college track stars who qualified for
the 200-meter race at the 1968 Olympics in Mexico City.
They thought about boycotting the Olympics because of
racism and injustice in the world.

They decided to run the race and show the world what they believed. Tommie and John came in first and third; Tommie broke the world record. They stood on the Olympic podium without shoes as a symbol of poverty. They wore beads and scarves around their necks in memory of lynching victims, and they raised black-gloved fists to show unity and strength.

On a college campus in Spartanburg, South Carolina, the astronomer Maria Mitchell looks through a telescope.

As a child on Nantucket Island, Maria loved to climb to the roof with her father to look at planets and stars. In 1847, while sweeping the night sky with her telescope, she discovered a new comet.

No one believed a woman could discover a comet until astronomers in Italy confirmed that Maria's comet was real. The comet was named "Miss Mitchell's Comet."

In a park in Napa, California, Dolores Huerta and Cesar Chavez stand tall.

Growing up in California, Dolores and Cesar saw their parents and other migrant farm workers struggling because of bad working conditions and low pay.

They organized strikes and started the United Farm Workers movement in 1962. Cesar and Dolores persuaded millions of Americans to stop buying grapes until farmers started treating workers fairly.

Now in her nineties, Dolores still speaks out for workers' health and safety. Her motto is "*Si, se puede!*" which means "Yes, we can!" in Spanish.

In Ping Tom Park in Chicago, Illinois, Judge Laura Cha-Yu Liu carries a law book.

In kindergarten Laura learned English. At home she spoke Mandarin with her parents, who had immigrated from Asia.

Laura was a top student at college and law school. As a judge she was the first Chinese American elected to public office in Chicago, in 2012, and the first Asian American on the state's appellate court.

She never forgot the excitement of learning English as a five-year-old. Thanks to Laura, courtrooms in Illinois provide interpreters and have signs in many languages.

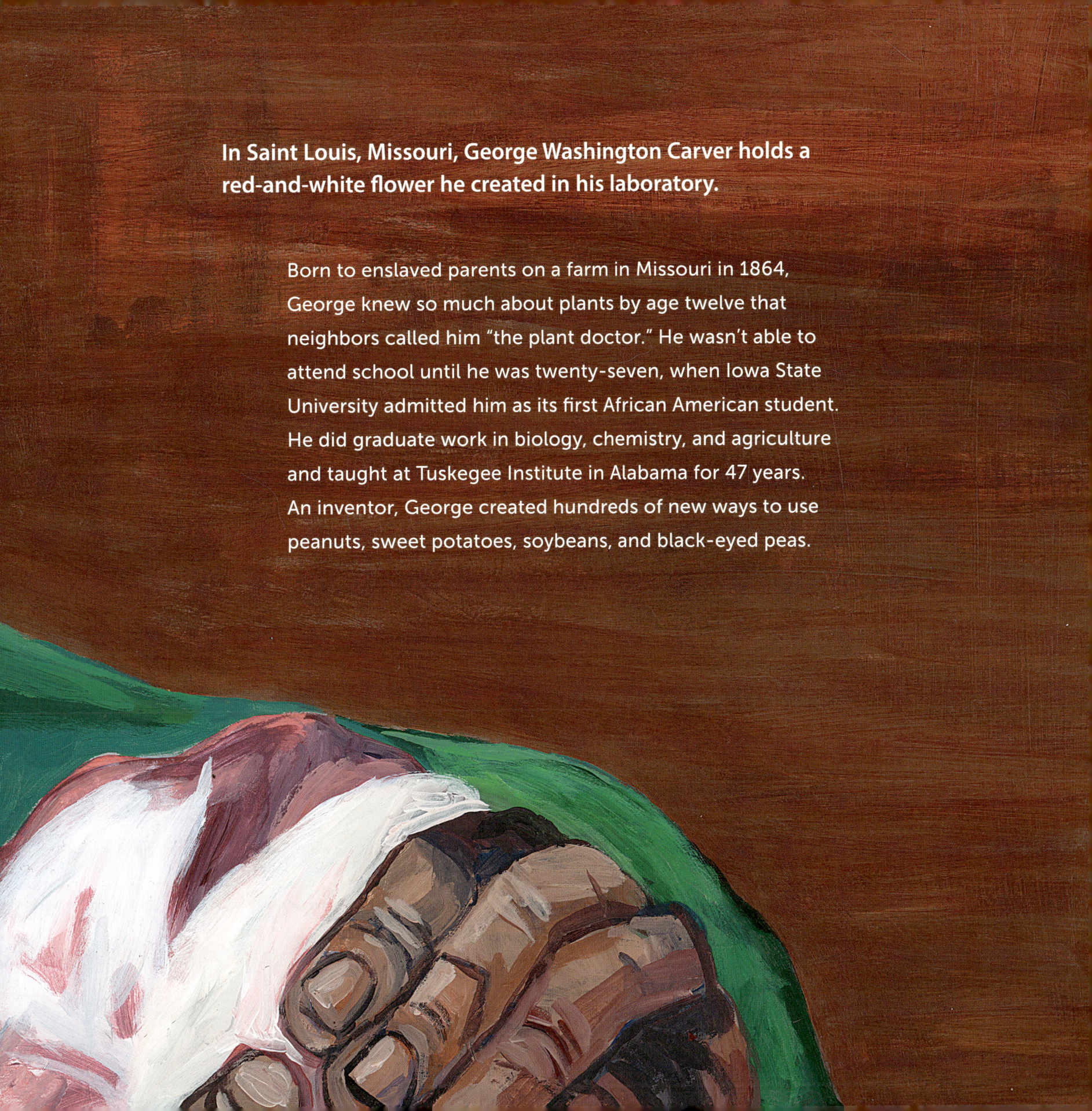

In Saint Louis, Missouri, George Washington Carver holds a
red-and-white flower he created in his laboratory.

Born to enslaved parents on a farm in Missouri in 1864,
George knew so much about plants by age twelve that
neighbors called him "the plant doctor." He wasn't able to
attend school until he was twenty-seven, when Iowa State
University admitted him as its first African American student.
He did graduate work in biology, chemistry, and agriculture
and taught at Tuskegee Institute in Alabama for 47 years.
An inventor, George created hundreds of new ways to use
peanuts, sweet potatoes, soybeans, and black-eyed peas.

At the airport in Austin, Texas, Barbara Jordan is deep in thought.

Barbara had a big voice for a little girl. She recited poems, sang in choirs, and became a champion debater in high school and college. Her powerful voice resonated in the halls of the Texas State House, where she was the first African American woman state senator, and resounded in the nation's Capitol. In 1972, she was the first African American woman from the South ever elected to the House of Representatives.

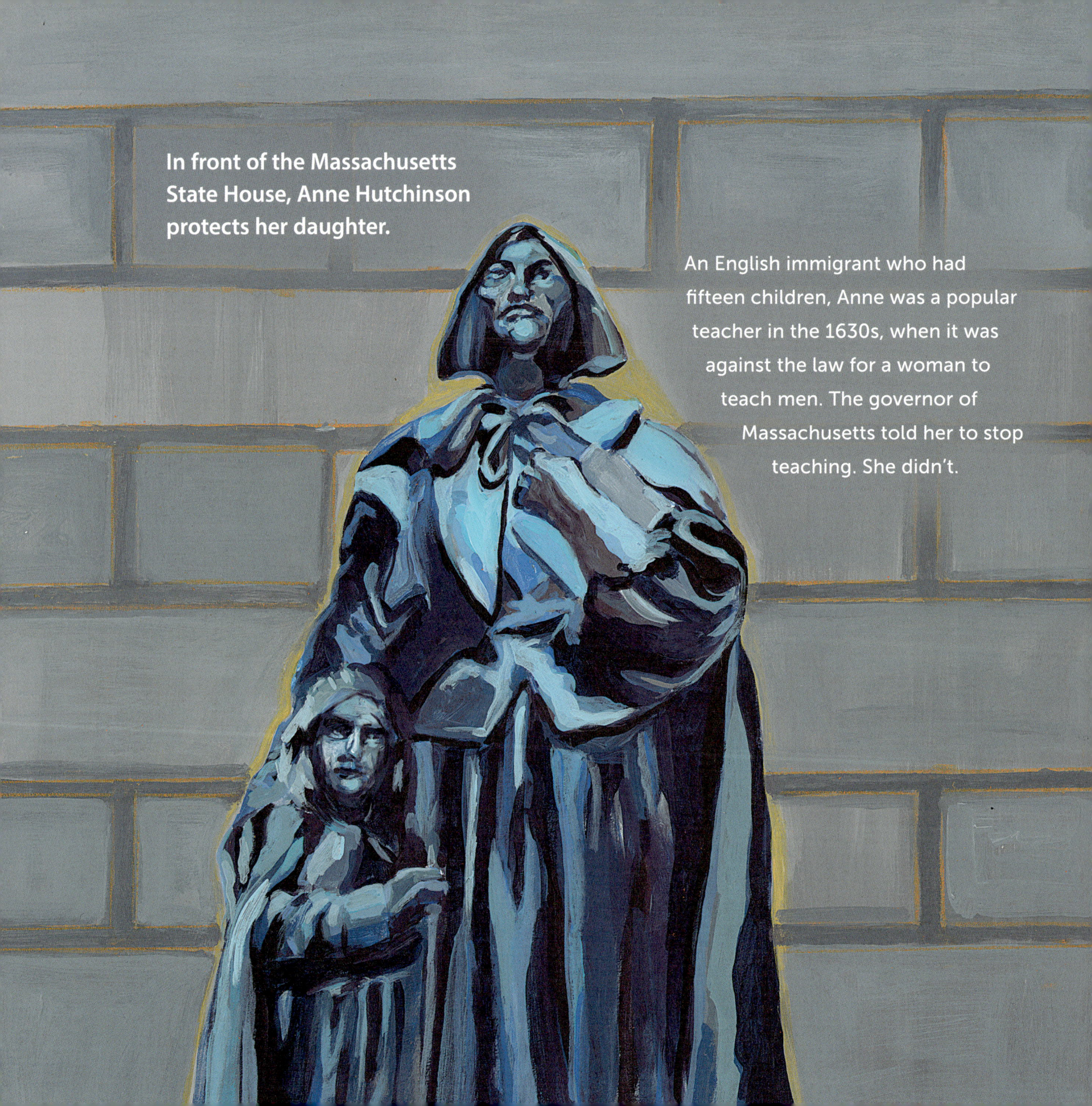

In front of the Massachusetts State House, Anne Hutchinson protects her daughter.

An English immigrant who had fifteen children, Anne was a popular teacher in the 1630s, when it was against the law for a woman to teach men. The governor of Massachusetts told her to stop teaching. She didn't.

The governor and more than
thirty judges, all men, brought her to court, tried
and convicted her, jailed her, and kicked her out
of Massachusetts for teaching men.

With her family and friends, Anne walked sixty
miles to a settlement she started on Rhode Island,
where she continued to teach.

In a garden outside Miami, Florida, Marjory Stoneman Douglas tells a story about her book, *Everglades, River of Grass*.

Marjory was a journalist who loved the Everglades, a beautiful part of Florida filled with animals and birds. She wrote her book so the Everglades would be protected and preserved. In 1947, a year after her book came out, the Everglades became a national park.

In Lincoln Park in Washington, D.C., Mary McLeod Bethune hands a book to a child.

Ten-year-old Mary had to walk two hours to school in South Carolina. At home she taught her older siblings, who couldn't go to school. Mary loved teaching so much she opened a small school in Florida in 1904. That school became Bethune-Cookman College, one of just a few colleges then that admitted African Americans.

Back at the Capitol Building, another statue of Mary McLeod Bethune was dedicated in 2022 by the state of Florida.

Thanks to a law passed in 2000, states can now switch their statues.

In many states, people are changing their minds about whose contributions should be honored.

Kansas recently replaced one of its statues with the aviator Amelia Earhart, the first woman to fly nonstop across the United States.

Alabama added a statue of Helen Keller, a deaf and blind girl who learned to talk with her hands and grew up to travel the world speaking out for equal rights.

Who else needs a statue in the Capitol?

What other stories can we tell? Who will tell them?

What other brave Americans helped make the world a better place?
Do they need a statue, too?

Compendium

This story is happening right now. Across the country, statues in public places are being added and subtracted.

The 100 statues in the Capitol collection are gifts from the 50 states. The first statue was dedicated in 1864 and placed in the National Statuary Hall. By the 1930s the hall was crowded with heavy statues. Now, because of their weight, the statues are spread out in prominent locations around the Capitol Building.

In 2000, the year that Congress first allowed states to replace their statues, 90 of the 100 statues depicted white men.

Sarah Winnemucca's birth name, Thocmetony, means *shell flower* in Paiute. No one knows when Thocmetony took the name Sarah. She worked as an interpreter and negotiator, gave more than 300 speeches, and opened a bilingual school. Her bronze statue was made by Benjamin Victor and dedicated in 2005.

Every year on June 11, crowds gather around **King Kamehameha's** statue to honor him with music and dancing. They decorate his statue with leis made of Hawaiian flowers. His statue was made by Thomas Ridgeway Gould and dedicated in 1969.

In 1920, as a member of Congress, **Jeannette Rankin** helped draft the Nineteenth Amendment to the Constitution, which gave women the right to vote. A peace activist, she voted against entering World War I and World War II. In 1968, when she was 87, she led 5,000 women on a march protesting the Vietnam War. Her bronze statue was made by Terry Mimnaugh and dedicated in 1985.

One of the world's leading women scientists, **Dr. Florence Sabin** published 39 books and articles. After retiring from Johns Hopkins University, she moved home to Colorado and continued working for public health. Her bronze statue was made by Joy Buba and dedicated in 1959.

Barbara Johns, 1935–1991

The statue of Barbara Johns, designed by Stanley Bleifield and dedicated in 2008, is part of the Virginia Civil Rights Memorial in Richmond.

After starting the strike at her school, Barbara Johns worked with other students, teachers, and lawyers from the National Association for the Advancement of Colored People to bring a lawsuit against the school board and the county. The lawsuit was denied, but later, in combination with similar lawsuits, it went all the way to the Supreme Court and became part of the historic 1954 case, *Brown v. Board of Education of Topeka*.

Some people attacked Barbara Johns for her role in ending school segregation. The Ku Klux Klan burned a cross on her yard. To protect her, her parents sent her to Montgomery, Alabama, to live with her uncle, a civil rights activist named Vernon Johns. Barbara Johns will soon receive a statue at the Capitol, from Virginia.

Deborah Sampson, 1760–1827

Deborah Sampson was a fighter not only in war but also for equal rights. After discovering she was a woman, the Army refused to pay for her service or grant her a veteran's pension. With a husband and three children to feed, she asked the Massachusetts Legislature for her pay and pension. The state agreed because of her "extraordinary female heroism," but she still didn't receive the federal veterans' pension. She wrote to the United States Congress asking for equal treatment. In 1805, for the first time, Congress ordered the military to pay a pension to a woman. More than 200 years later, Congress passed the Deborah Sampson Act to assist women veterans.

The statue of Deborah Sampson, made by Lu Stubbs and dedicated in 1989, shows her in uniform, holding her musket, hat, and powder horn.

Tommie Smith, 1944–, and John Carlos, 1945–

On October 16, 2005, thirty-seven years after Tommie Smith and John Carlos made their silent protest at the Olympics, their statue, made by an artist named Rigo 23, was dedicated on the campus of San Jose State University. Students had petitioned for the statue to honor the Olympians and their professor, Harry Edward, who had founded the Olympics Project for Human Rights in 1967.

After the race at the 1968 Olympics, the runner who placed second, an Australian named Peter Norman, showed his support for Tommie Smith and John Carlos by wearing an Olympics Project for Human Rights pin while standing on the podium. Asked if he wanted to be represented in the statue, Peter Norman suggested his spot be left empty so visitors could stand for justice with the Americans.

Maria Mitchell, 1818–1889

Maria Mitchell was America's first professional female astronomer. Her statue, made by Elliot Offner and dedicated in 2004, stands in front of the science building at Converse College in South Carolina.

Colleges did not accept women during her youth, but in 1865 a new college for women called Vassar made her its first professor of astronomy. She taught at Vassar for the rest of her life.

The comet she discovered in 1847 is still known as "Miss Mitchell's Comet."

Dolores Huerta, 1930–, and Cesar Chavez, 1927–1993

Dolores Huerta and Cesar Chavez both grew up speaking Spanish among migrant farm workers in California. By the time Cesar Chavez dropped out of school at age twelve to help support his family by picking fruit full time, he had attended thirty different schools. Dolores Huerta attended college and became a teacher, but seeing so many hungry farm children in her classroom convinced her to become a union organizer.

The United Farm Workers movement they started in 1962 relied on nonviolent tactics like marches and fasts to bring attention to farm workers' struggles. In 1966, to publicize a six-month strike by Mexican American and Filipino grape pickers in Delano, California, they walked 280 miles to the state capitol. By the time the marchers reached Sacramento, the movement had won its first union contract.

The statues of Dolores Huerta and Cesar Chavez in Napa, California, were made by Mario Chiodo and dedicated in 2015.

Laura Cha-Yu Liu, 1966–2016

In 2017, one year after Judge Laura Liu died of cancer at 49, a life-size bronze sculpture of her made by Eric Blome was dedicated in a park in Chicago. It was the city's first statue of a woman.

As the child of immigrants, Laura Liu was sensitive to the needs of people who do not speak English as a first language. She always had translators in her courtroom so everyone understood the words being spoken, and sometimes stopped a trial to make sure a translation was correct.

George Washington Carver, 1864–1943

In 2005, a statue of George Washington Carver made by Tina Allen was dedicated in the George Washington Carver Garden at the Missouri Botanical Garden in Saint Louis.

George Washington Carver revolutionized farming in the South by introducing plant diversity, crop rotation, conservation, and natural fertilizers. He taught farmers to feed hogs acorns rather than commercial feed, and to enrich croplands with swamp muck rather than artificial fertilizers. He encouraged them to plant a variety of crops to heal soil depleted by centuries of cotton farming, and developed hundreds of new uses for these crops. From peanuts alone he made 300 new products, including milk, cooking oil, and soap.

Barbara Jordan, 1936–1996

In the summer of 1974, as the Judiciary Committee of the House of Representatives considered the impeachment of President Richard Nixon, Barbara Jordan captivated millions of Americans. "My faith in the Constitution is whole, it is complete, it is total," she said in her opening remarks, televised across the nation. "I am not going to be an idle spectator to the destruction of the Constitution."

Barbara Jordan's statue was made by Bruce Wolfe and dedicated in 2002 in the Barbara Jordan Terminal at the airport in Austin, Texas.

Anne Marbury Hutchinson, 1591–1643

Anne Hutchinson's statue stands in front of the Massachusetts State House, a few blocks from where she lived in Boston nearly 400 years ago. Sculpted by Cyrus Dallin in 1915, the statue was paid for by women seeking the right to vote, which Congress granted them through the Nineteenth Amendment to the Constitution in 1920.

At first no one wanted the statue. The Boston Public Library refused to accept it. The Massachusetts Legislature gave the statue a spot on the State House lawn but would not dedicate it. The statue was finally dedicated in 2005.

The only woman ever to cofound an American colony, Rhode Island, Anne Hutchinson is one of our nation's founding mothers.

Marjory Stoneman Douglas, 1890–1998

Marjory Stoneman Douglas devoted much of her long life to protecting and restoring the Everglades. She fought sugar companies that wanted to drain the land for plantations, and real estate speculators who wanted to sell it for development.

"There are no other Everglades in the world," she began her book *Everglades, River of Grass*. A grassy marshland covering most of Florida's southern half, the Everglades is home to thousands of species of animals and birds, many endangered. It supplies fresh water to millions of residents of South Florida. It contains the sovereign homelands of Seminole and Miccosukee Indians. It is the only subtropical wetland left in the nation and one of the largest wetlands in the world.

Her statue, made by Freda Tschumy, was dedicated in 2005 in a botanical garden near Miami.

Mary McLeod Bethune, 1875–1955

 Born in South Carolina to parents who had been enslaved, Mary McLeod Bethune was a political activist and organizer who is remembered as the First Lady of Struggle. She worked closely with Eleanor Roosevelt and became president of the National Council of Negro Women.

The statue of her in Lincoln Park was made by Robert Berks and dedicated in 1974 on the 99th anniversary of her birth. The first statue of an African American woman erected on public land in Washington, D.C., it shows her sharing her love of learning with children.

In 2022, when Florida dedicated a statue of her in the Capitol Building, Mary McLeod Bethune became the first African American honored by a state in the collection. The sculptor was Nilda Comas.

Text copyright © 2024 Eve LaPlante and Margy Burns Knight
Illustration copyright © 2024 Alix Delinois
Design Copyright © 2024 Frame25 Productions

Hardcover ISBN 978-0-88448-951-1 • Library of Congress Cataloging-in-Publication has been filed and is available at catalog.loc.gov

 TILBURY HOUSE PUBLISHERS™

2395 South Huron Parkway Suite 200 Ann Arbor MI 48104
Printed in the United States.

10 9 8 7 6 5 4 3 2 1